Words
On
Pages

1999

Stephanie Jacobson

Contents

Contents
(con't)

Contents
(con't)

Contents
(con't)

snowfall

The snow outside is falling
and icicles form
on the window ledge
Frost
has gathered
on the glass
but the bitter cold
does not touch me
I can't even feel the chill
of the wind
as it whips by
Seems I haven't felt much
of anything
for the longest time now
If only I could
reach out
Feel the sting of the
frozen air
just
feel
something

good days

What it would be like
To have good days again
To not be sick
Just this once
To have purpose
To have meaning again
To just get out of
This bitter darkness
And feel warmth
I haven't felt warmth in
So long
What is it like
To not be sick
Day in and day out
To have a 'good' day
...whatever that is
To have the energy
To live for one day
Just one day
And not be exhausted
By the time it's over
But I'm so tired
So very tired
There is nothing left in me
But to curl up here
On the floor

wish

I wish I knew what to tell you
What to do to make your pain disappear
Some magic words
Or touching gesture
To take your hurt away
Your eyes tell a thousand stories
Of losses
Of let downs
Of shattered dreams
They miss that sparkle they once had

like her

I wish I was like her
The pretty one who caught your eye
And stole your heart
I wish I was like her
And had 'beautiful breasts
With nice meaty nipples'
For you to enjoy
I wish I was like her
With a nice round ass
For your hands to explore
And whose lips taste sweet
I wish I was like her
The one who wants to be your angel
And fall asleep with you
God, I wish I was like her
Then you'd love me again

kitty cat

Curious thing you are
Eyes attentive
Catching every little detail
Ready to pounce at any given moment
Queen of your domain
Black midnight satin you are
Tufts of white like clouds
On a black sky
Give you character
And what a character you are
What an interesting creature you are
So regally you sit
Perched in your chair
Head held high
Your gentle hum is soothing
You stretch and roll over
So content to lay there
Belly wide out
I wonder what you think
As you stare off into the room
"I bet if cats could write,
They'd write great poems"
I say
You thump your tail and nuzzle my face
Agreeing with me

chuck

Grant got a monkey cup today
It's a red monkey cup
With a straw built into the handle
The monkey cup has a white plastic top
He looks like a sailor in a little white hat
He's a 'Sippin' Safari' monkey cup
He's a fat little monkey
But he's happy
With big happy monkey eyes
And a little happy monkey smile
It would have been cuter
If they used his tail for the straw handle
But they didn't
He does have a curly monkey tail though
That's very important in a monkey, you know
He's from Elk Grove, Illinois
I didn't know they had monkeys in Illinois
Surprise, surprise
Cuz Grant got a monkey cup today
And named his monkey cup Chuck

tiny goddess feet

I worship her
tiny goddess feet
her smooth skin
like honey
I lazily run my tongue
over her
luscious toes
swim in her
sweet embrace
I am delirious
drunk
on her beauty
I ache to
pleasure
such a
vision of womanly beauty
hair smelling of peaches
I lust after a
thousand moments together
with her
my girl
who sings
like a
whispering summer breeze
I kneel at her
tiny goddess feet
she
is
my
eternity

pleasure

I worship her
the luscious goddess
at her perfect feet
drunk from her
sweet passion
swim in her beauty
I am weak
from loving her
she who whispers
to me a
delicate language of
pleasure

she

she
is
your
friend
with
the
delicate
nipples
sweet
lips like
honey
perfect ass
I could
never
be as
gorgeous
as
her

delicate beauty

you dance before me
delicate beauty
swaying back and forth
your long blonde hair
falling
gently
over your
creamy white
shoulders
vibrant crystal blue eyes
are innocently daring

penthouse

I want to pose for Penthouse
In some exotic place
A white sandy beach
A deep blue sea
In the background
To compliment
The naked female form
All of its curves and
Its beauty
Would it turn you on
To see me
Splayed out across
The glossy pages
For all the world to see?

I-86/porn store

They're gonna close our porn store
And the truck stop
And our post office
The flea market
And the Tomahawk
And the Plantation Motel
Everything's gotta go
For I-86
All because of one
Stupid light in the
Middle of the highway
What a dumb place for a stop light
If you took out that light
That would solve the problem
Instead they're gonna
Build a cloverleaf
Or interchange
To get from Lowman to Wellsburg
(right across the highway)
And in the process
They'll tear up half our town
So much for Lowman
Cuz they're gonna close our
Porn store
For I-86

hometown

So, where do you live?
In Lowman.
Where?
Y'know Lowman? Right off the highway? By the
crossover there?
Where?
Down by where Coldiron's is, y'know? Where the flea
market is?
Oh! By the porn store?!
Yeah. By the porn store.

leather pants

For some reason
It takes confidence
To wear leather pants
And the confidence you feel
Wearing them is
Amazing
The mixture of the
Sateen lining
And the leather pant leg
Is new to me
And nice to me

blonde goddess

My angel
My blessing
My whole world
That's what you are
My blonde goddess
My Barbie doll
Perfect, to me
In every way

dependency

we become so
dependent
on others that we
forget
how to function on our
own when the time
has to come
it's like learning to live
all over again
dependency is a
dangerous thing
you forget how to
be yourself,
by yourself,
for yourself

women

what's wrong with
finding women attractive?
What's wrong with
Finding beauty in
their curves
soft, delicate skin
long, shapely legs
balanced perfectly
on tiny feet in
black stilettos
thick ruby lips
long lashes
golden hair

tourist attraction

Everything around here
Is so drab and dead
The trees have lost their leaves
Grass has turned brown
What's left of the snow
Has turned gray
From the roads
Cars are covered in salt
And look so drab
Even the sky has lost
It's radiant blue
I can't believe this place
Is a tourist attraction

prisoner

Hiding
As I always have
Avoiding confrontation
The house is dark
I'm alone
Shut up in my room
A prisoner
Of myself
My heart races at
Every sound
A door slamming
A car driving by
Is it her?
Has the time finally come?
Maybe I should go
I should run
And avoid
And hide
Like I always have
I pour a glass of orange juice
Which ends up on
The kitchen floor
I don't even notice the
Shaking of my hands
As I wait
Like a prisoner ready for
Execution
Just get it over with
Please

something special

You ask me if there's
Something special
I'd like
And I don't know
How to
Answer you
I don't know
What is special
Anymore
Is special a lot of
Money spent?
Is special a moment
That lasts for a lifetime?

special

What do I want
That's special?
I'd love to be
showered in
tokens of your
appreciation
Or given flowers
every week
To be wined and dined
and treated
like a queen
But I'm perfectly content
with a Burger King
dinner
A night at the mall
And gas money
for the drive home

perfection

What does it mean to
Be perfect?
Is perfect thin?
Is perfect beautiful?
Does perfect have blonde
hair and blue eyes?
Does perfect have big
round breasts?
Is perfect smart?
Is perfect funny?
Is perfect rich?
Does perfect have a
great job?
Does perfect drive a
nice car?
Does perfect live in
a big house?
Does perfect have
a significant other?
And are they perfect, too?
Is perfect happy?
Is perfect perfect?

my own

I want a place of
My own
Of our own
With our personal touches
My own styles
Combined with yours
Creating a
Whole new style
Unique in
Every way
A place for us to call
Home
Together

tired

I am tired
So very tired
A nap would be
A tease at
This point
But it would be
So refreshing
Right now
But there are
Too many things
I need to do
Before I can
Fall asleep

directionless

Where will I be in ten years?
If only I knew
I can't even tell you
Where I'll be tomorrow
It feels like I have
No focus
No goals
To work towards
And I'm just taking up space
Do what you love
But what I love
Is not solid
Writing isn't going to get
Me a 9 to 5 job
Not one that I love
So what do I do?
Do I settle for something
And hope it grows on me?
Do I hope for the best?

today

Jamie got a little frog
With googly eyes
Holding a heart
Today

Grant got a little monkey
With a big monkey smile
That's holding a heart
Today

Steffi got...
Steffi got...
Steffi got the satisfaction
Of making
Her friends happy
Today

out loud

It's bad enough I've got to
Have one of these written
And read for class
But why would I want
To subject myself to
That ridicule
That humiliation
On my own time?
If I read these
Out loud
Are they going to
Mean more?
Are they going to be
Understood better?
Are you even going
To listen?
Why would I want to
Subject myself
To that?

this place

This place
Is slowly
Sucking
The inspiration
Out of me
Drab
Plain
Walls
Florescent lights
Stale air
Droning
Nagging voice
Fake voice
I have
Nothing
To offer

explain

How do I tell you
What's going on
In my head
So you'll understand?
How do I explain
To you
That I'm not happy
With who I am
With what I am
And that I don't know
What to do to change it?
If only you could see me
The way I see me
In my head
What I see
When I
Look in the mirror
If only I could see me
The way you see me
I just wish I knew
What that way was

fake

They pay me to be fake
To smile pretty
Be friendly
And to act like I enjoy
Cleaning up after you people
That I'm happy
Picking up your dirty dishes
Refilling your coffee cups
And explaining what's
On our buffet

They pay me to be fake
At $5.15 an hour

you, too

You do it, too
Y'know
That condescending
Bitter tone
When you address
Someone
So don't pin that shit
All on me
Maybe it's not how
Things are said
More than how
Things are heard
Instead

just hungry

Tacos sound good
Right about now
A nice hard shell
Overflowing
With lettuce
And cheese
And
The best fake ground beef
They please all the
Senses
Eyes are pleased by
The mixture
Of the greens,
Yellows,
Oranges and
Browns
The touch takes in
The texture of the shell
Taste, well taste
It pleases quite well
By a quick mix of the
Four food groups
The crunch is a lovely
Sound heard by the ear
And the smell of the grease
On the grill completes

Or, maybe I'm just hungry

wait

Wait...
I just wrote a poem
About a taco-
How sad is that?
I guess all literature
Doesn't have to be
Deep and meaningful, eh?

made for pleasure

Women are made for pleasure,
Aren't they?
Isn't that the way we were
Brought up?
To look pretty for the boys,
Always do as you're told
A living doll
To be dressed up
And made pretty
Like you're supposed to be
You are subservient
And he is your master

block

Why won't it come?
What I need
And oh, how I
Need it
I sit and wait
To receive
Hands open
Mind open
Heart open
Why won't it come?

run out

Seems I've run out of
Inspiration
The thoughts
The words won't come
You try to block out
All sound
But it doesn't work
Try to find rhythm
In the chatter
But nothing's there
The inspiration is gone
Nothing left now
But to sit and wait
For it to return

art

What a sight you are
So pleasing to the eye
I could lose myself in
You for hours
Those deep brown eyes
That rose petal smile
Your blonde hair flowing
Across your shoulders
A work of art

everyone

Everyone tells me how thin
I'm getting
And how great I look
But I don't feel it
I feel tired and slow
I don't feel thin
But I suppose that's self-esteem
Or the lack thereof

it

There are bills to pay
A car to fix
Work to be done
But I don't seem to
Have the time
Yet I have all the
Time in the world
The money is there
I just don't have it

empty page

An empty page
Soon filled with words
Written in ink
Someday to be read
And reread
A few words get changed
Here and there
And then the page
Doesn't seem so
Empty anymore

sleep

If I could only take a
nap
just curl up into a
little ball
all tucked in nice
and warm
and fall asleep
and not be here

wonders

She wonders
If he's happy
With her
If she still turns
Him on
If her breasts
Are big enough
Does she please him
Is his mind on
Something
Someone
Else

how

I wish I knew
Hot to talk to you
How to tell you
What's on my mind
How to ask you
What's on your mind
I'm so afraid
Of saying the
Wrong thing
Of starting an
Argument
Of making you mad
Of making you
Hate me

good times

He sits at a table
Sipping his beer
Watching her dance
Naked
Her tits in his face
She just wants to
Make a few bucks
He just wants to
Fuck her

outsider

I wonder why
We don't share anymore
We don't sit and talk
About what's on our minds
What's bothering us
What makes us
Mad
Happy
Sad
We don't share
What we do
In a given day
Who we talk to
What we talked about
Where we went with them
We don't share
What we write
Whether it's an essay paper
Or a piece for
Ourselves
I don't feel like
A part of your life
Because I don't know
What you do
Yet you expect me
To share every little detail
Of my day with you
And I hear nothing of yours

show you

I wish I could show you
Everything that I write
But I don't know
If you care what it says
What little interest you have shown
Has been fleeting
And quickly passed
And you've got better things
To do with your time
I'm afraid to ask you
To read anything
For fear that you'll turn
Me down
Or that you'll say yes
And not mean it
And just throw all of this aside

hate

i hate myself
i hate who i am
what i am
how i look
how i think
how i laugh
how i cry
the way i feel
i manipulate
i lie
i hate my lack of ambition
of creativity
of inspiration
of patience
of understanding
of trust
i hate the fact that i'm shy
that i'm weak
that i'm self-centered
that i'm depressed

girlfriend

I wish I knew what
I meant to you
If you trusted me
If I was someone
You couldn't live without
If I was someone
Important in your life
Now and forever
Or if I'm just another
Girlfriend

graceful

Graceful as she walks
Towards me
This beauty with
The golden hair
Her spirit seems so
Wild and free
Causing all
To stop and stare

penis

I have no penis
I can't change my flat tire
I can't go to strip clubs
I don't enjoy porn
I can't piss outside
Or standing up, for that matter
I have no penis
So I actually
Think
With my brain
And don't have the urge
To fuck every girl with
Big tits who walks by
Cuz I don't have a penis

monday evening

The truckers sit next to me
Speaking in their redneck drawl
Swappin' motors
Stallin' diesels
I smoke my menthol cigarette
Drinkin' coffee
Eaves droppin'
The waitress comes to
Warm up my cup
Sucks to be her
Stuck in a place like this
That southern drawl
Is addictive
My companions play hangman
And the truck drivers leave
I light another cigarette
And ponder my
Existence

frank zappa

Vince told me he
Went to Ohio
To see the face
Of Jesus on the
Side of a water tower
He looked at the rusty water tower
And saw a face
Not Jesus
But Frank Zappa
The only one who really saw
God that day
Was a 15 year old boy
Selling souvenirs mugs

coulda been

I coulda been a contender
I coulda been somebody...

Maybe in some other life
I was great
Probably a man
With a penchant for
Thick red wine
and a good Cuban cigar
Who had a way
With the ladies
And a one-liner or two
For the boys at the bar

vestal

I wish I were still in Vestal
I didn't have to worry
About running into people
I try to avoid
I didn't have to hide
Who I really want to be
We acted as silly and childish
As we wanted to
Cuz we could
Cuz we didn't have to worry about
Running into someone we knew
Not even a day back in town
And already I feel the stress
Start to build
Back up

myself

I'm tired of being fake
Pretending to be
Something I'm not
Just to please somebody
To please everybody
But myself
Leaving town for the day
Made me realize
How unhappy I've been
How unhappy I've made myself
By trying to be
Something I'm not
I'm finally ready to make
A change
Be who *I* want to be

fear

My greatest fear
Is losing you
Not being able
To feel the joy
You bring into
My life
Anymore
To not have you there
To comfort me
In your arms
When I need you
The most

band of silver

A band of silver
Around my finger
Such a simple little token
Means so much
The day we met
You gave this to me
And I've been yours
Ever since

satin sheets

I lay you down in satin sheets
And velvet rose petals
Your blonde hair
Splays out on the pillow
As you dreamily gaze into
My eyes
Your pale porcelain skin
In contrast to
The black midnight satin

who i am

Shall I rediscover who I am?
Should I dye my hair with
Colorful streaks?
Wear silver rings
On my fingers
On my toes
One through my eyebrow
And one through my navel?

surrender

Your smooth velvet skin
Under my tongue
The bitter salt of your sweat
Is my treat to feast on
I trace your curves
Dancing across you
You laugh lightly
And I feel your laughter
Reverberate through you
Your insatiable smile
Peers down at me
As I gently
Please you
You're like a child
In my arms
As you surrender yourself
To me

tony

Daydreaming
The hours away
As Mr. Bennett
Croons In the background
"Fly me to the moon
And let me play among the stars..."
It's not the words he sings
It's how he sings them
Such passion
Such sincerity
Such beauty

aisle

Someday
You and I
Will be the ones
To walk down
That aisle
You in your tuxedo
I in my white dress
To solemnly swear
To honor
Love
Obey
And cherish
One another
Forever

friendship

You've stuck by me
Through thick and thin
Even through the times
I pushed you away
No matter how many times
I fell flat on my face
You were there
Waiting in the wings
To pick me back up
And dust me back off
You sat back and watched me
Destroy myself
And everything around me
Yet never let it ruin
You and I
And for that I thank you
That's the true meaning of friendship

in your arms

I fell asleep
In your arms
Last night
My head resting
On your broad chest
Listening to your heart beat
And soothed by the
Rhythm of your
Breathing

the way

It's the way
Your blonde hair
Falls across
Your
Broad shoulders
And dances against
Your bronzed skin
The warmth of your
Hazel eyes
The gentle touch
Of your strong hands
The child-like innocence
Of your smile
That makes me
Love you so

if only

If only I could
Reach out
Touch you
Hold you
Feel your body
Close to mine
To smell your cologne
And nuzzle your neck
Run my hands
Across your broad chest
Feel your arms
Wrap around me
Hold me close
Keep me safe

in my dreams

You were in my dreams
Last night
As subtle as a breeze
At times
But you were there
I could feel your touch
Taste your kiss
Hear your voice

100th poem

My 100th poem of the year
Should be
Spectacular
Marvelous
Awe-inspiring
And great
TV shows have grand celebrations
For their 100th episodes so why should my poem
Be any different?
Let's throw a party
And celebrate an occasion
A little over
4 months
In the making
Here's to 100 more

parking lot

I sit in the parking lot
Contemplating
Wondering
I butt another cigarette
Into the concrete
I've picked myself up
And dusted myself off
A thousand times
Before you
And I don't need to
Feel sorry
Any more

unfurnished apartment

I sit on the floor
In an unfurnished apartment
Head slightly buzzing
From the alcohol
Throat raw from chain-smoking
Head thick with
Fatigue

why?

Why can no one love me?
For who I am
For who I am not
My good traits
And my bad
Why can no one
Enjoy my company?
Enjoy my conversation?
I am not beautiful
Not by your standards anyway
But why?
Why can't I be respected?
Given a little credit
And not be treated
Like I'm stupid?

save me

I feel
as though
I'm falling
slowly down
into the
dark abyss
crying out
for someone
to save
me but
no one
does

disenchanted

I feel helpless
Hopeless
Worthless
Abandoned
Alone
That there should be more
To my purpose
My reasoning
For my existence
For my...

too far away

sitting in a coffee shop
too far away from home
nibbling on grease-laden fries
as I try to wake up
in need of a shower
clean clothes
and a nap
a day before Thanksgiving

deacon blues

my mind draws a blank
as a chill falls over me
steely dan on the radio
singing ''Deacon Blues'
The trip to Syracuse was unnecessary
And costly

"They have a name for the winners in the world,
And I want a name when I lose..."

mistletoe

I feel like
I'm wasting your time
By being here tonight
I just wish
Someone could understand
Would understand
Where I was
Coming from
And where I am
Going to
Today of all days
Alone on this highway
One more time
I ask of you
To sit with me
And understand
And understand
And stand under
The mistletoe
And wait for me
I'm the one who's wings are
Clipped
And can't afford to fly

cleveland marriott

the skyline was all
hazy and gray
the day we arrived in town
me
with my bright yellow streaks
and muddy black boots
you
with your designer jeans
and the T-shirt you stole
from the strip club last night
what a sight we were
walking into the lobby
of the Marriott in Cleveland
you with your designer luggage
trimmed in leather
me
with my beat up duffle bag
over one shoulder, and my
black satchel on the other
you're not a materialistic person,
you once told me
I'd like to think I am,
I responded

cuervo gold

you asked me
what it is
that I could be
a casual drunk
while you were stuck
being a lush
I muttered something
About genetics and
Will power and other
Such gibberish
In between mouthfuls
Of tequila

steve

again
here I am
traveling down
that same stretch of highway
I've traveled before
Too far away from home
My sole companion
On the journey
A middle-aged trucker
Named Steve
He says we have a lot in common
I say I need to get off
At the next town
With a Denny's
Where I'll sit and
Drink coffee
Find a place to crash
For the night
And head back out
The next morning
Down that same stretch of highway

lullaby

driving along
the highway
steady rhythm
in the thump of the
tires
combined with the
hum of the engine
is my lullaby
as I light another cigarette
and roll down the window
to try and wake up

the half of it

"You're lookin' pretty rough, my friend,"
You tell me as I sit down
Next to you
And your polished black boots
"You don't know the half of it,"
I respond
As I reach for a cold one
And rock in the rhythm
Of the crack of the pop-top
And watch in awe of
The cool smoke
Billowing from the hole
Before paying homage
To my patron saint

get gone

I just need to
Get out
Get over it
Get on with my life
I ain't got time
For these games
Anymore
I'm tired of playing
I just want to sleep

my place

I wish I knew what
My place was
What spot,
If any,
I hold
In your life
If you value me as a friend
Or if you value me
As something more

goodnight

and there you are
and there you have it,
folks
nothing more
nothing less
than your average
display
of teen-age angst
take it for what it's worth
take it for more
than what it seems
take it for granted
like you do to me

SHORT & SWEET

loving you

deliriously mad
with passion
I am weak
from
loving you

* * *

me

How do you perceive me?
Do I turn you on?
Is there something I can change?
Should I just leave things alone?

* * *

interest

I often wonder
If you read my
Writings
Just to humor me
Or if you are
Really interested
In what I have to say

spectacular

You are spectacular
All of you
And you don't know it
It's in your walk
In your voice
In your smile

∗ ∗ ∗

empty

Languidly
She lays there
Void of life
Of love
Wanting his
Embrace

∗ ∗ ∗

velvet

her voice was
velvet
when she told him
she lied

untitled

Delicate beauty
Gentle as the morning dew
After dawn's rain

* * *

object

women are nothing
but whores
to you
they are
only here
for you
to screw

* * *

favorite past time

he watches her
breasts
heaving before him
her ass swaying
in his face
she is his wet dream

vivid

she
with her
vivid beauty
dancing
in the rain
for everyone to see

* * *

scream

I scream but
No one listens
So I become quiet
And cry

* * *

good & drunk

What I wouldn't give
For a night
To get
Good and drunk

* * *

sex

Sex is a
Sacred embrace
Between two

she is beauty

Translucent champagne
Butterfly goddess
Eyes
Of stars
Porcelain skin
She is beauty

* * *

seductress

I sit here
Next to my seductress
Her low cut dress
A tempting sight

* * *

wildflower

Beautiful woman
Swaying in the summer breeze
My wildflower

* * *

embrace

Delicate beauty
I am weak from loving you
Sleep in your embrace

red dress

Her red dress
Clings to her body
Like a glove

* * *

wanting

I want to run my
Fingers through your
Long black hair
I want to run my
Hands across
Your broad chest

* * *

whisper

Whisper
Softly
Your voice like
A breeze
Drifting
Through
The clouds
On butterfly wings

beautiful

I lay in your arms
And feel beautiful
And happy

* * *

hunger

My lips yearn
For a sweet taste
Of yours
My body hungers
For your touch
My heart aches
For your love

* * *

dance of love

The satin sheets
Are drenched in sweat
Drenched in the
Scent of you
Sharing in my passion
In our dance
Of love

last night

I dreamt of you last night
Laying in my bed
So full of passion
And desire
Laying in my bed
With another

www.ingramcontent.com/pod-product-compliance
Lightning Source LLC
Chambersburg PA
CBHW032014040426
42448CB00006B/635